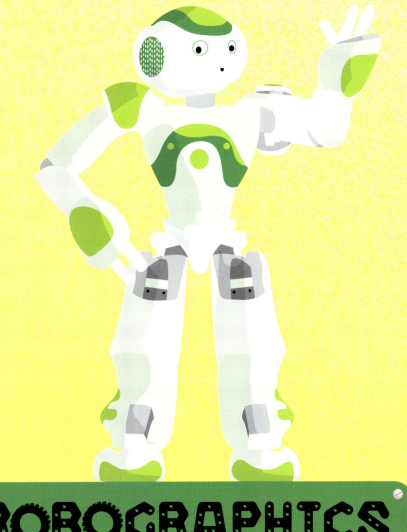

ROBOGRAPHICS

SUPER-SMART ROBOTS

CLIVE GIFFORD

WAYLAND

First published in Great Britain in 2022 by Wayland
© Hodder and Stoughton, 2022

Credits
Artwork: Collaborate Agency
Design: Collaborate Agency
Editor: Nicola Edwards

ISBN 978 1 5263 1593 9 (hb); 978 1 5263 1594 6 (pb)

Printed and bound in China

Picture credits:

The publisher would like to thank the following for permission to reproduce their pictures:

AIRBUS: 13

Getty Images: ROB LEVER/AFP via Getty Images 4

Nvidia: 5

Shutterstock: Olga Bugrow 21; catwalker 18; Anton Gvozdikov 27; Phonlamai Photo 29; Sundry Photography 15

Wikimedia Commons: 19, 26

Every attempt has been made to clear copyright. Should there be any inadvertent omission please apply to the publisher for rectification.

The website addresses (URLs) included in this book were valid at the time of going to press. However, it is possible that the contents of addresses may have changed since the publication of this book. No responsibility for any such changes can be accepted by either the author or the Publisher.

Wayland, an imprint of
Hachette Children's Group
Part of Hodder and Stoughton
Carmelite House
50 Victoria Embankment
London EC4Y 0DZ

An Hachette UK Company
www.hachette.co.uk
www.hachettechildrens.co.uk

CONTENTS

SUPER-SMART SOLUTIONS

Robots already perform much valuable work. Super-smart robots and other devices are being developed to do a whole lot more! Building smarter robots is about equipping machines with the abilities they need to work better by themselves and perform varied and complex tasks.

2,000,000 ...

... the number of hours Brain OS cleaning robots had worked by August 2020, all without human supervision.

Taiwan's IVS (Intelligent Vision System) robot plays chess and can recognise letters to play word games like Scrabble. This research robot learns to identify objects and what it can do with them from their shape, colour, size and location.

Vision system identifies type of chess piece and works out moves.

Twin grippers adjust force based on how heavy and delicate an object is.

BRAINY UPGRADE

Some increasingly smart bots rely on boosts in computing power. NVIDIA's Jetson Xavier NX computer module (above) for future robots is smaller than a credit card but as powerful as a supercomputer!

CLEVER DESIGN

Giving robots more clever sensors and the ability to learn in new ways can also make them smarter. A NAO robot, for instance, can learn a task by mimicking what people do and then storing those actions in its memory.

50+ ...

... the number of sensors packed inside a 58 cm-tall NAO robot.

NAO

21,000,000,000,000 ...

... the number of calculations this 70 x 45 mm computer can make per second.

Sensors include:

25 joint sensors

10 touch sensors

Ultrasonic sensors

4 microphones

Infrared sensors

2 HD cameras

Gyroscope for balance

INDEPENDENT INTELLIGENCE

Early robots relied on costly and slow computers, some the size of an entire room. Once computers soared in performance, shrinking in size and cost, it meant robots could be equipped with powerful computing to run complicated programs.

All the power of a giant 1970s mainframe computer can now be found on a silicon chip the size of your fingernail.

SMART BOT TIMELINE

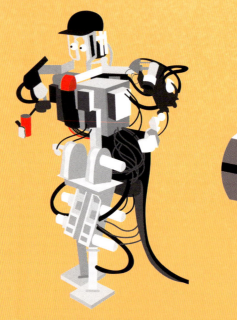

1921
The word "robot" is first used in Karel Čapek's play *R.U.R: Rossums Universal Robots.*

1961
First robot put to work – the Unimate robot arm, used in car factories.

1973
WABOT-1, the world's first full-sized smart humanoid robot, created in Japan.

1985
A PUMA 560 becomes the first robot to assist in a medical operation.

BETTER THAN US?

Robots can be built to be stronger and able to work for longer than people. They can be more accurate than us, able to repeat the same task to within a fraction of a millimetre time and time again. When these abilities are linked to an intelligent robot's ability to learn, the results can be impressive.

Toyota's sharpshooting CUE3 robot uses sensors in its chest to measure distances. Its joints send feedback signals to its computer controller. This precisely adjusts the angles of the joints so that the robot makes the basketball shot accurately each time.

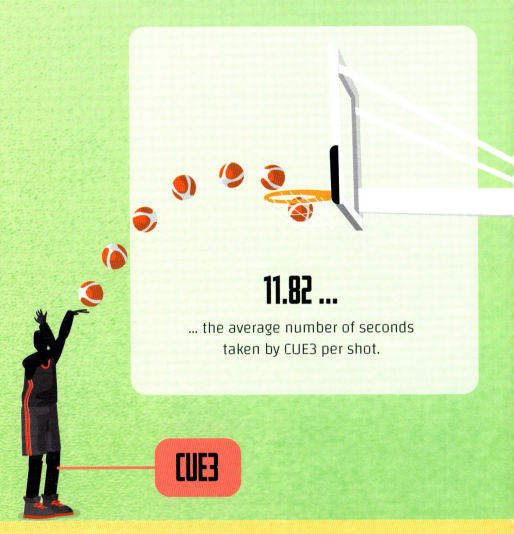

11.82 ...

... the average number of seconds taken by CUE3 per shot.

CUE3

1997

IBM Deep Blue computer beats human world chess champion, Garry Kasparov.

2005

Stanley driverless car navigates 281 km-long off-road course with no human help.

2011

IBM's Watson wins an episode of the US TV quiz show *Jeopardy*.

2019

CUE3 sets record for number of successful basketball shots in a row (2,020 shots).

SOCIAL BOTS

Advances in artificial intelligence and cloud computing are allowing robots to understand speech and access a wealth of information over a computer network. There's a long way to go before a robot becomes your best friend, but some machines are getting sociable.

Yeoboseyo

Konnichiwa

Hola

Hi

Merhaba

WHAT DID YOU SAY?

Most social robots can respond to some spoken commands. To understand more complex conversations, some bots send a person's speech to a cloud computing site where the words are analysed. Keywords and instructions are sent back to the robot to act upon.

21 ...

... the number of different languages the Elias robot foreign language learning app from Finland can recognise. Designed for use with the NAO robot, the program can recognise Korean, Turkish, Japanese and English words, amongst others.

LEKA

LIKEABLE LEKA

Not all social robots need to be chatty. Leka plays educational games and interacts with children with learning difficulties using movement, sound, vibration and lights to grab their attention.

Camera tracks faces at a rate of 30 frames per second.

KIKI

Facial recognition software identifies owners and their friends.

PAWS FOR THOUGHT

Zoetic AI's Kiki robot is a cat devised by robotics expert Mita Yun. As it spends time with its owner, the robot learns and develops its own personality which can be shy, rebellious, loyal or affectionate. Kiki can be taught new tricks and remember when something she does is liked or disliked.

Speakers allow Kiki to emit a growl if a new person approaches her.

Microphones can recognise owner's laughter. Kiki will remember what she did to make her owner laugh and attempt it again, later.

Dimensions: 28.7 cm x 15 cm x 16 cm

16 ...

... the number of touch sensors located all over Kiki, allowing owners to pat, tickle and cuddle the robot.

Screen allows Kiki to display various simple facial expressions including boredom, joy and fear.

GETTING EMOTIONAL

Robots don't have real emotions, but some can give responses that appear emotional. For example, a robot might appear sad and regretful if it is told off sharply. The long-term aim is to create robots which people find to be natural and effective companions and colleagues.

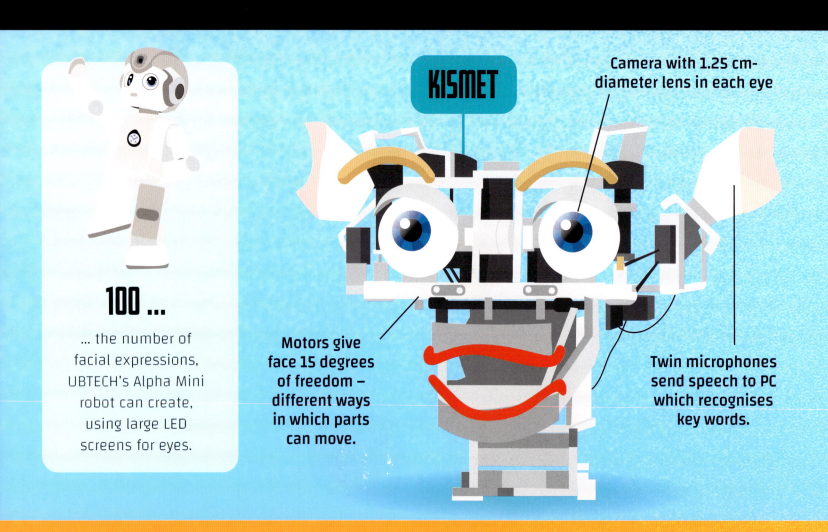

100 ...

... the number of facial expressions, UBTECH's Alpha Mini robot can create, using large LED screens for eyes.

KISMET

Camera with 1.25 cm-diameter lens in each eye

Motors give face 15 degrees of freedom – different ways in which parts can move.

Twin microphones send speech to PC which recognises key words.

POUTING PIONEER

Built by Cynthia Breazeal in the 1990s, Kismet was one of the first robots to express emotions physically. Multiple motors moved its eyelids, eyebrows, mouth and ears to form facial expressions. The robot viewed and listened to a person and attempted to respond with a suitable expression.

HAPPY

SURPRISED

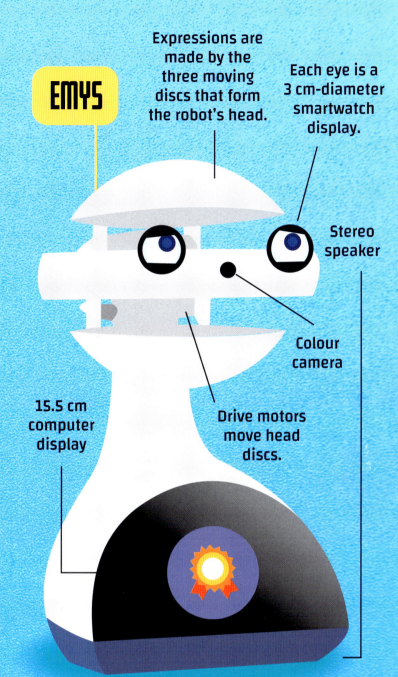

EMYS

Expressions are made by the three moving discs that form the robot's head.

Each eye is a 3 cm-diameter smartwatch display.

Stereo speaker

Colour camera

15.5 cm computer display

Drive motors move head discs.

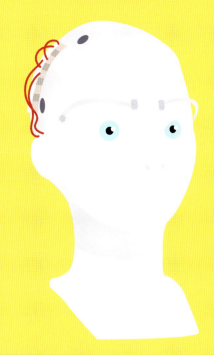

The **Simulative Emotional Expression Robot (SEER)** from Japan uses motion-sensitive cameras. These track human facial expressions as people pass by, which the robot then copies.

MIND YOUR LANGUAGE

Developed in Poland, EMYS is a foreign language teaching robot for young children. The 4 kg, 37.5 cm-tall bot expresses emotions including surprise, irritation if its base is pushed and delight if a child gets a new word right.

4 ...

... the number of touch-sensitive areas on EMYS's head. If stroked, the robot responds by smiling.

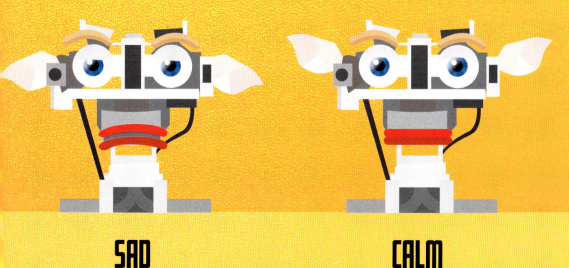

SAD

CALM

9 ...

... the number of emotions Kismet could display: happiness, sadness, anger, surprise, tiredness, fear, sternness, disgust and calm.

PERSONAL ASSISTANTS

Robotic assistants, powered by artificial intelligence, are expected to be one of the most important branches of robotics in the next 20 years. Able to access massive databases, such intelligent assistants could make work easier, faster and more accurate - and leisure time more fun!

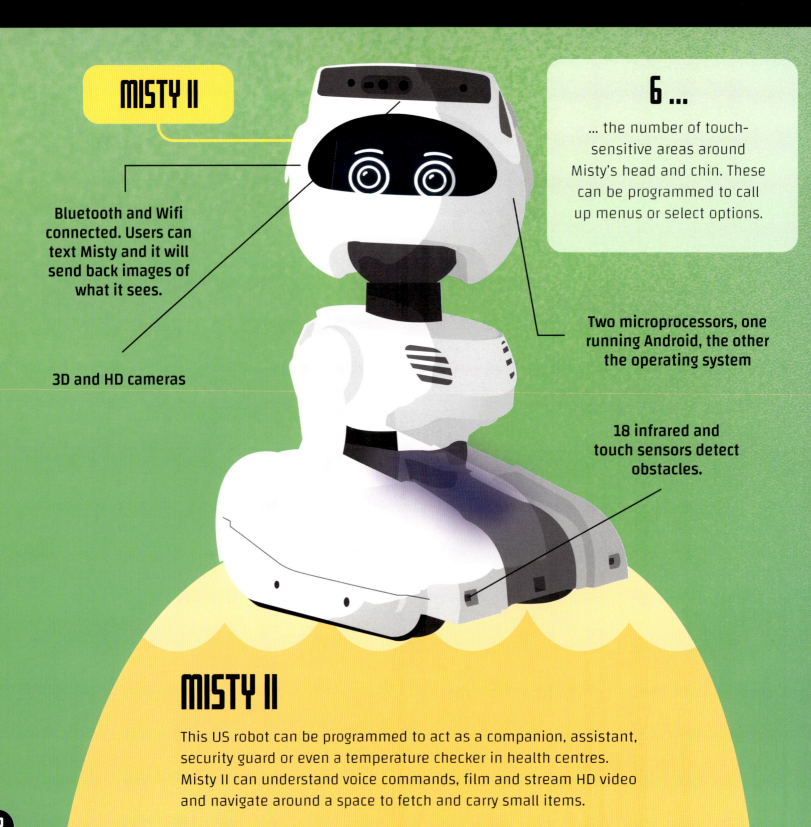

MISTY II

Bluetooth and Wifi connected. Users can text Misty and it will send back images of what it sees.

3D and HD cameras

6 ...

... the number of touch-sensitive areas around Misty's head and chin. These can be programmed to call up menus or select options.

Two microprocessors, one running Android, the other the operating system

18 infrared and touch sensors detect obstacles.

MISTY II

This US robot can be programmed to act as a companion, assistant, security guard or even a temperature checker in health centres. Misty II can understand voice commands, film and stream HD video and navigate around a space to fetch and carry small items.

SPACE SIDEKICK

In 2019, a floating astronaut assistant blasted off into space on board a SpaceX Dragon spacecraft. The ball-shaped Cimon-2 from Germany assists astronauts on the International Space Station (ISS) by reading out instructions, answering queries and giving reminders.

7 ...

... the number of emotions, CIMON-2 can detect in astronauts' speech: excited, frustrated, polite, rude, sad, sympathetic and satisfied. The robot can alter its tone of speech in conversation.

Robot's 14 fans move it around and let it shake and nod its head to questions.

Cameras film experiments and are used for facial recognition.

Diameter:
32 cm

Weight:
5 kg

Battery life:
3 hours

Mission duration:
3 years

Total cameras:
7

Location:
400 km above Earth

Speakers broadcast messages, text instructions, and even play music.

Robot communicates with a cloud computing centre on Earth. This processes face and speech recognition data and beams the results back up to the robot instantly.

9 microphones detect sound above the constant 72 Db noise of the ISS (a noise level equal to a vacuum cleaner).

DRIVERLESS VEHICLES

Many AGV (automated guided vehicle) robots travel around factories, hospitals and offices ferrying supplies. Out on the road, though, there's a lot more to contend with. Robotic road vehicles need complex arrays of accurate sensors and powerful controllers to be safe and drive themselves autonomously – without any human supervision.

0-5 ...

... the levels of vehicle automation, with level 5 being completely autonomous. Levels 1 and 2 give a human driver electronic aids, such as parking assistance. Level 4 means the vehicle does all the driving but controls exist for a person to drive if they prefer.

ROBORACE

360° camera provides all-round views.

282.42 KM/H ...

... the top speed of Roborace, the world's fastest autonomous car, achieved in 2019.

1,000,000,000 ...

... the estimated lines of computer code needed to control a single level 5 (completely) autonomous car, according to Jaguar Land Rover.

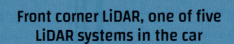

Front corner LiDAR, one of five LiDAR systems in the car

SAVING LIVES AND THE PLANET

Most road accidents are the result of human error, such as those caused by tiredness or dangerous driving. Driverless cars reduce these threats and their sensors and controller can react quicker to sudden situations, potentially saving thousands of lives. They may also save fuel or electricity by driving in more energy-efficient ways.

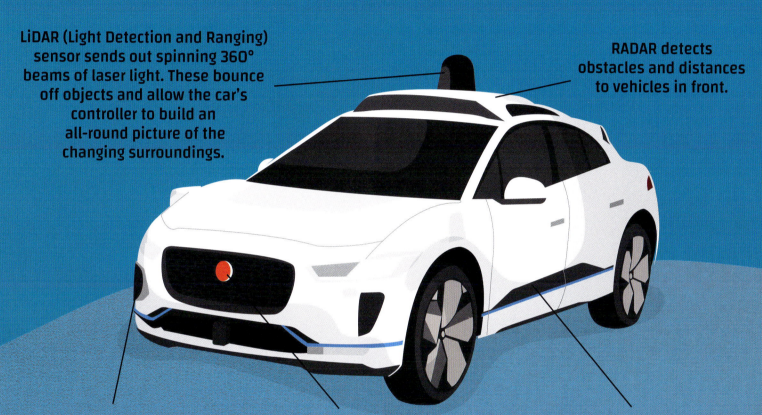

LiDAR (Light Detection and Ranging) sensor sends out spinning 360° beams of laser light. These bounce off objects and allow the car's controller to build an all-round picture of the changing surroundings.

RADAR detects obstacles and distances to vehicles in front.

Infrared sensors detect lane markings, pedestrians and cyclists.

Cameras provide images interpreted by the car's controller to identify obstacles as well as kerb edges, traffic lights and signs.

Ultrasonic sensors fitted to sides and rear of car work over short distances when parking.

29 ...

... the number of cameras in a Waymo car. These enable the vehicle to spot a stop sign up to 500m away.

32,000,000 ...

... the number of kilometres driven by Waymo driverless vehicles on US public roads by early 2020.

PROBLEM SOLVERS

To be really useful as machines that work by themselves, robots have to be good at problem-solving. They need to be able to identify what the problem is, and then decide if they can tackle it or if they need to alert human helpers. This all takes machine intelligence.

SPOT THE SOLUTION

Boston Dynamics' Spot robot is a nimble four-legged robot with potential uses in construction, search-and-rescue, healthcare and other fields. In development, the robot learned how to climb uneven steps, map its surroundings and open doors.

Length: 1.1 m

Total weight: 30 kg

Cost: US$ 74,500

Able to carry extra sensors, gas detectors or other loads of up to 14 kg.

DOOR TO DOOR

Many companies are getting excited about using driverless vehicles for deliveries but the problem of how to get the packages from the street to the front door remains. Agility Robotics' Digit may provide an answer. This two-legged robot walker folds up inside the rear of a driverless van, then unfurls itself | to carry a package to a door.

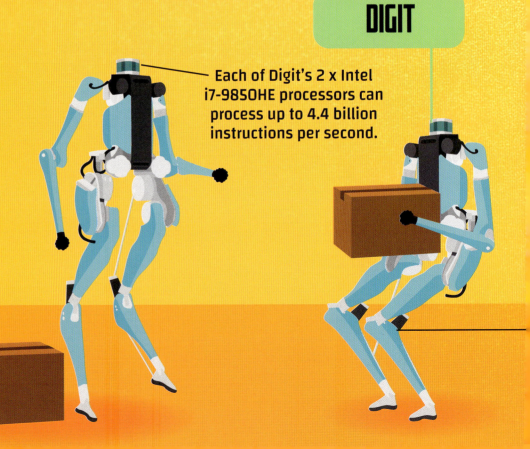

DIGIT

Each of Digit's 2 x Intel i7-9850HE processors can process up to 4.4 billion instructions per second.

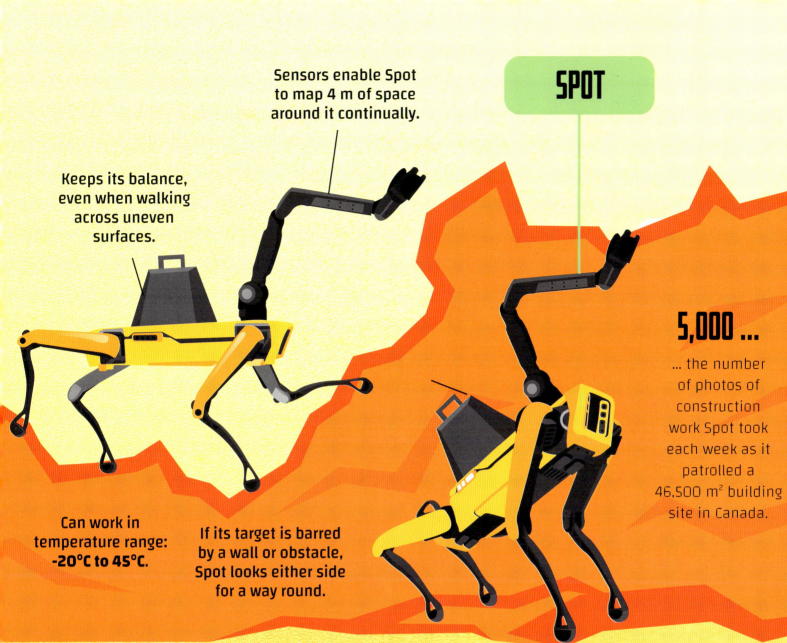

Sensors enable Spot to map 4 m of space around it continually.

Keeps its balance, even when walking across uneven surfaces.

5,000 ...

... the number of photos of construction work Spot took each week as it patrolled a 46,500 m² building site in Canada.

Can work in temperature range: **-20°C to 45°C.**

If its target is barred by a wall or obstacle, Spot looks either side for a way round.

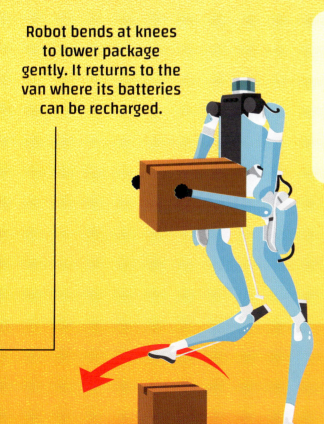

Robot bends at knees to lower package gently. It returns to the van where its batteries can be recharged.

18KG ...

... the maximum parcel weight Digit can carry (42% of its own body weight).

LiDAR and other sensors help plot a path away from obstacles.

ROBOTS LIKE US

Ever since robots were first thought about, people have been fascinated with making machines in their own image. Humanoid robots have to work incredibly hard to match basic human abilities, including balancing, movement and recognising and handling objects.

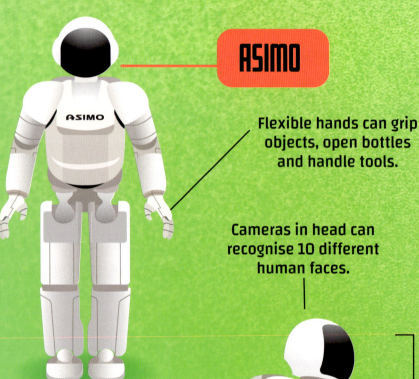

ASIMO

Flexible hands can grip objects, open bottles and handle tools.

Cameras in head can recognise 10 different human faces.

STAYING BALANCED

Walking on two legs and climbing steps are abilities we might take for granted, but they're no easy task for robots. They require serious processing power to achieve the same result. Honda's legendary ASIMO robot was the first humanoid to walk up stairs and run with ease, both forwards and backwards!

Height: 1.3 m

Weight: 54 kg

Walking speed: 2.7 km/h

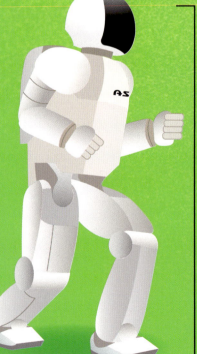

1.3 m

Asimo can run at a speed of 9km/h. It would take Asimo 4 hours, 42 minutes to run a marathon.

The robot's twin cameras and controllers can predict a corner and, just like humans, lean the robot into the bend to keep its balance.

NO SWEAT!

Kengoro, built by engineers at the University of Tokyo, mimics the human body more closely than other humanoid robots. Motors pull cables to move Kengoro's fingers and other joints. Parts of the robot heat up during operation, so the robot is cooled by water flowing through tubes. Kengoro appears to sweat as some of the water evaporates through small holes in the robot's aluminum body.

Height:
1.7 m

Power consumption:
Up to 140 watts

Kengoro needs **half a glass of deionised (purified) water for cooling each day.**

Kengoro boasts 174 degrees of freedom, over 110 more than Asimo.

KENGORO

The **1.7 m-tall** Surena IV humanoid from Iran has **43 degrees of freedom** enabling it to dance, climb stairs, walk at **0.7 km/h** and handle all sizes of object, from this large beach ball to small power tools.

Five-digit hands and feet

The robot's parts are moved by 108 electric motors.

GAMES ROBOTS PLAY

Playing games may be fun, but for robots, computers and the researchers who work with them, it's a serious business. Many projects use strategy games to test a robot or computer's ability to learn, predict and react to events in order to make smarter decisions. This often involves analysing vast amounts of data.

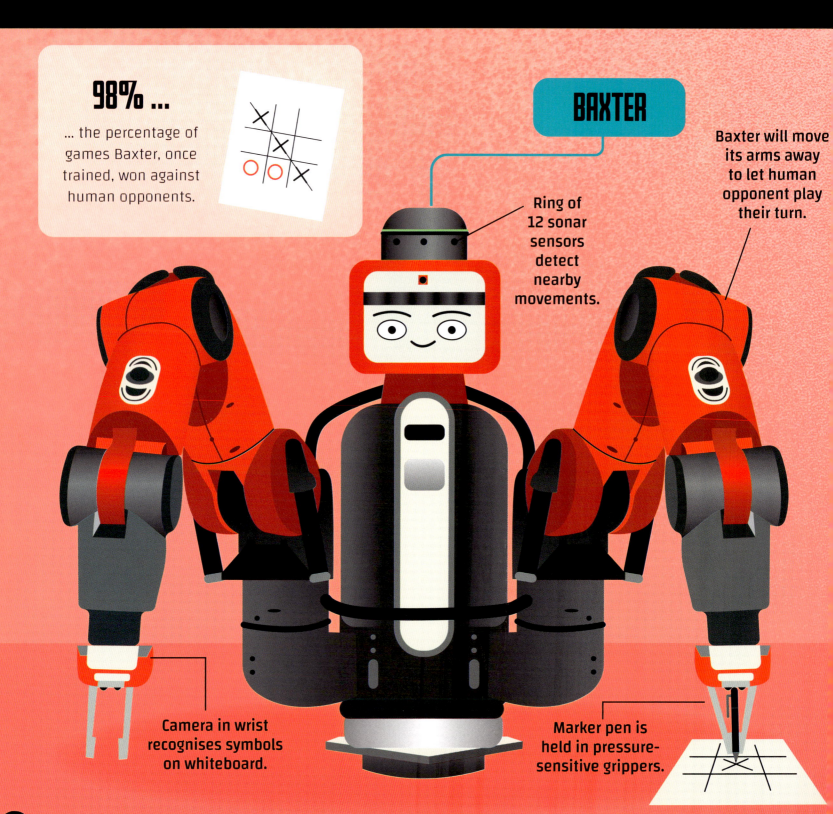

98% ...

... the percentage of games Baxter, once trained, won against human opponents.

BAXTER

Baxter will move its arms away to let human opponent play their turn.

Ring of 12 sonar sensors detect nearby movements.

Camera in wrist recognises symbols on whiteboard.

Marker pen is held in pressure-sensitive grippers.

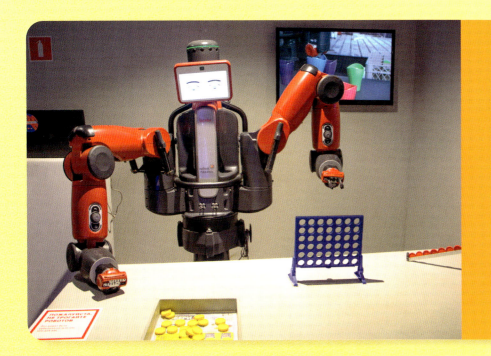

MACHINE LEARNING

A robot or computer that can learn the rules and tactics of games could be capable of learning many other things. That's why researchers equipped a Baxter robot (left) with a pen to play noughts and crosses. The robot trained itself in the best ways to play this and other games, such as Connect 4 (left), by trial and error.

ROBOCUP

There's much thinking as well as action in the RoboCup robotic football competition. The 2019 tournament, held in Australia, attracted 170 teams. Many took part in the 4-robot-a-side standard competition using Nao humanoid robots.

30 ...

... the number of decisions a RoboCup robot may need to make each second to track the ball, opponents and teammates and decide on its next move.

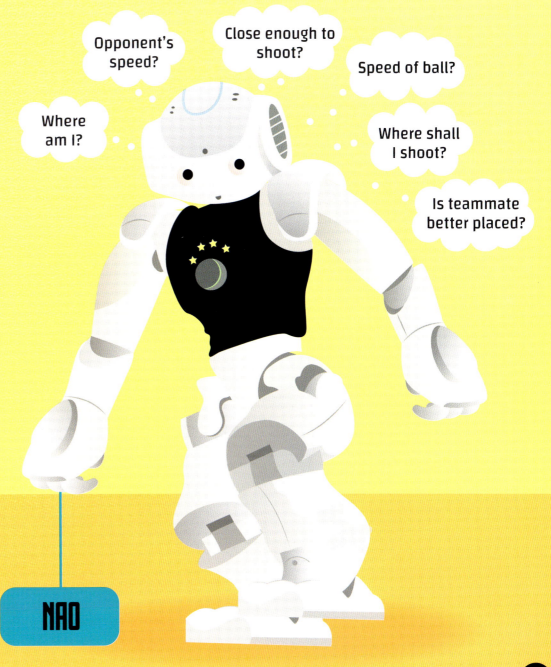

Where am I?

Opponent's speed?

Close enough to shoot?

Speed of ball?

Where shall I shoot?

Is teammate better placed?

NAO

BACK TO SCHOOL

Robots can be taught by uploading programs, containing thousands of lines of code, into their memory. It's also possible to teach a robot while it is running to perform the actions needed to complete a task. Just as robots can learn from people, so people can learn from building, programming and working with robots.

TEACH PENDANTS

These tablet devices allow a user to instruct a robot by moving it from point to point and performing actions all in a sequence. Each stage of the task is recorded and stored in memory so that the whole task can be repeated by the robot on its own again and again.

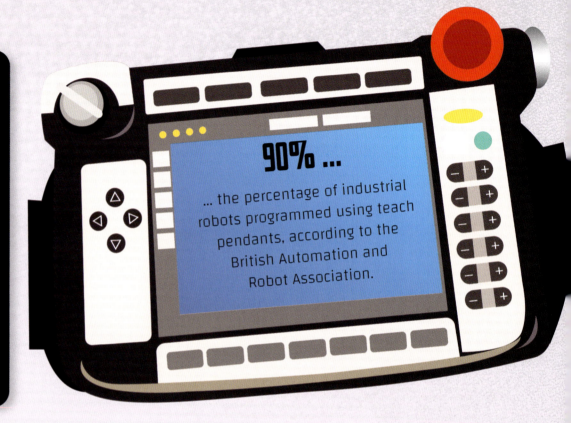

90% ...

... the percentage of industrial robots programmed using teach pendants, according to the British Automation and Robot Association.

ROBOTS TEACHING ROBOTS

Researchers at the Massachusetts Institute of Technology have created a knowledge base of how different objects can be handled by machines. When a human demonstrates a task, the robot accesses the knowledge base so it can perform the task itself. The robot can then teach the same task to another robot, even one of a completely different shape and size.

Two jointed arms with 16 degrees of freedom

Three-fingered grippers adjust force.

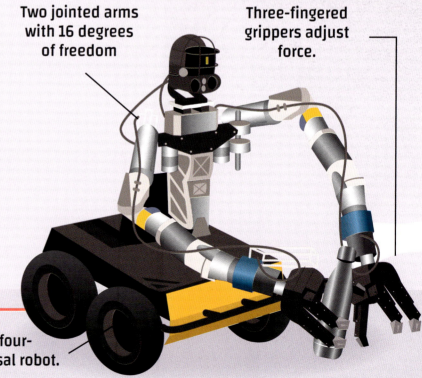

OPTIMUS

Optimus is a 99 cm-long, four-wheeled, mobile bomb disposal robot.

Having learnt how to pick up a metal flask containing chemicals, Optimus (below left) is now teaching Atlas how to do the same.

The robots communicate via radio signals.

87.5% ...

... the success rate of Optimus teaching Atlas tasks by itself in trials.

ATLAS

Atlas is a two-legged, 1.5 m-tall humanoid robot.

Hydraulic-powered joints give Atlas great flexibility.

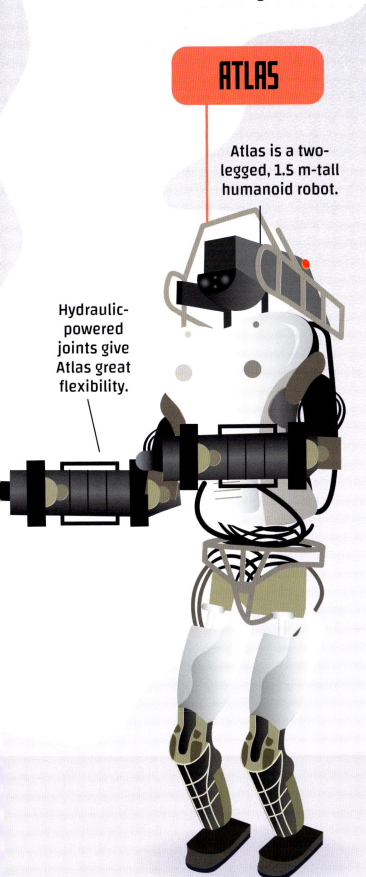

ROBOTS TEACHING PEOPLE

There's no better way to learn about robots than to build, program and operate one. Hundreds of different humanoid, wheeled and static educational robots allow users to modify bots and code new tasks.

Lego Mindstorms®

Krypton 3

Marty

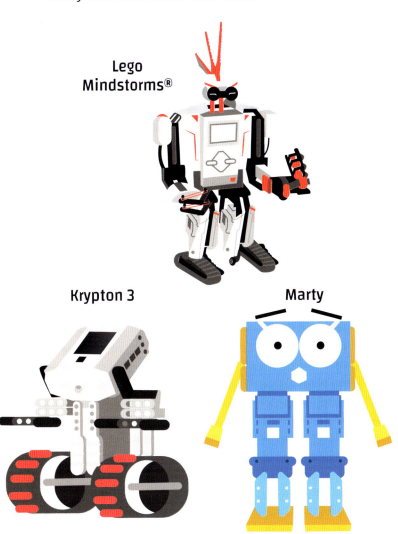

MACHINE LEARNING

For a machine to be artificially intelligent, it needs to be capable of planning, reasoning and solving problems. Machine learning is getting robots to learn by themselves from information they gather rather than people controlling them. Some robots can build their own knowledge bases or use trial and error to work out the best way to perform a task.

Clarke, a garbage-picking robot in Denver, USA, uses its controller and camera to learn what shape and colour recyclable objects are so it can gather them at a faster rate.

60 OBJECTS PER MINUTE

50% FASTER THAN HUMANS

Robot can climb 35 cm-high steps and 20-degree slopes.

LiDAR sensor sweeps the surroundings as robot builds up map of its environment.

100,000 ...

... the number of laser sensor measurements made by ANYmal C each second.

Controller plots path avoiding obstacles and calculates quickest route.

ANYMAL C

This four-legged robot handles masses of data sent back every second by its LiDAR and other sensors to map the space it is moving in. The robot can continually adjust its shape and leg position to suit the terrain, while plotting the best route to its target.

Weight: 50 kg

Dimensions: 105 cm × 52 cm × 83 cm

Top speed: 1 m per second

ANYMAL C

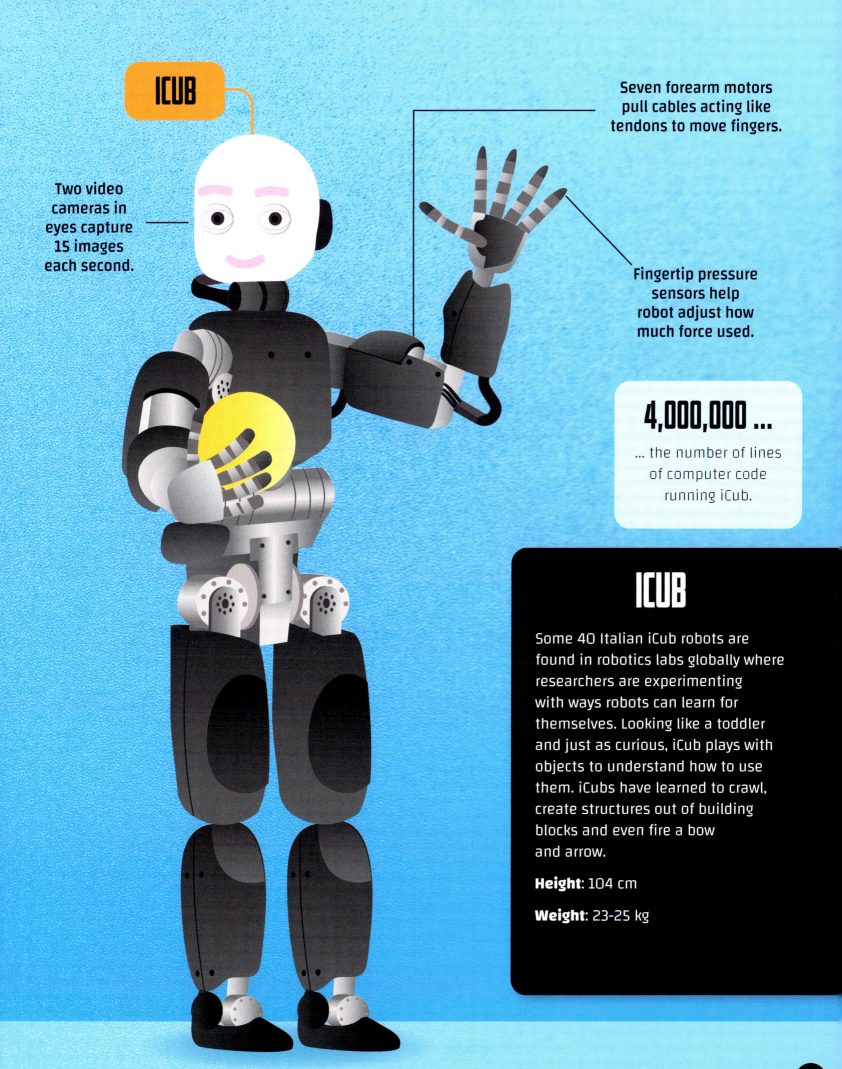

ICUB

Two video cameras in eyes capture 15 images each second.

Seven forearm motors pull cables acting like tendons to move fingers.

Fingertip pressure sensors help robot adjust how much force used.

4,000,000 ...

... the number of lines of computer code running iCub.

ICUB

Some 40 Italian iCub robots are found in robotics labs globally where researchers are experimenting with ways robots can learn for themselves. Looking like a toddler and just as curious, iCub plays with objects to understand how to use them. iCubs have learned to crawl, create structures out of building blocks and even fire a bow and arrow.

Height: 104 cm

Weight: 23-25 kg

ALMOST HUMAN?

Some humanoid robots have been built to look and act just like humans, even if they don't possess people's versatility and intelligence. These robots are used in media and public relations or to further research into artificial intelligence and how to make robots learn and act more like us.

The UK's Ai-Da robot (left) scans a scene via cameras in her eyes. Data from the images are run through a set of programming rules, called an algorithm, to create a jagged, abstract outline which is drawn onto the page by the robot. A human artist fills in the colour.

£1,000,000+...

... the money made so far from sales of Ai-Da's drawings and paintings.

SUPER SOPHIA

Few robots have given TED talks, appeared on TV chat shows or interviewed world leaders. But then, few robots are quite like Sophia. This Hong Kong humanoid robot uses AI to recognise and react to people's emotions from their facial expression and tone of voice. Sophia also uses natural language processing to try to understand questions and give a meaningful reply.

Gripping hands can hold range of tools including pencil with which she can sketch.

Lightweight aluminium arms contain many 3D-printed parts.

60 ...

...the number of facial expressions Sophia can make via **33** servos (electric motors) pulling cords attached to the inside of the facial skin.

In 2017, Sophia was both made a citizen of Saudi Arabia and the first non-human United Nations ambassador! She visited **38** countries in 2019.

16 ...

... the number of motors that move the face parts of humanoid robot, Jiang Lailai. This robot became a co-host of a science news TV show in China in 2019.

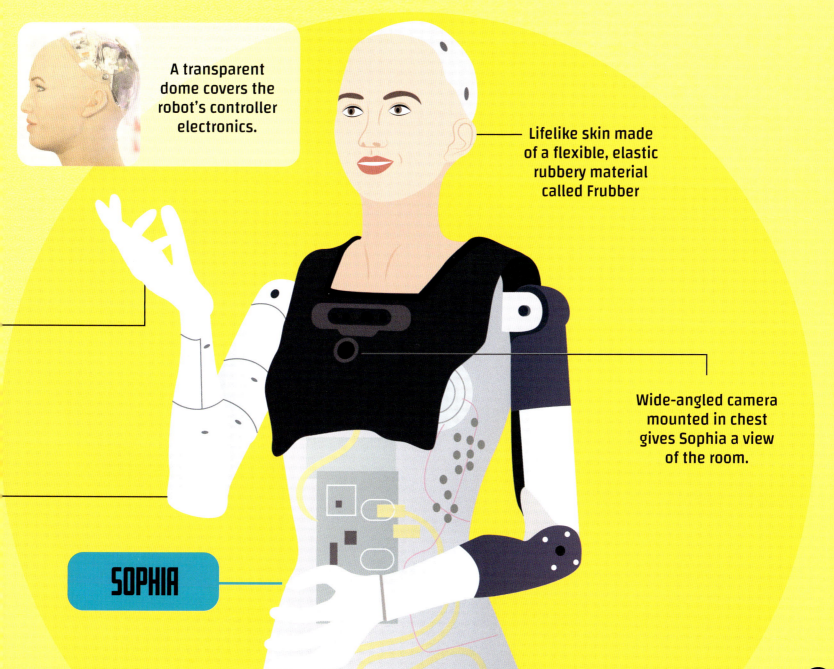

A transparent dome covers the robot's controller electronics.

Lifelike skin made of a flexible, elastic rubbery material called Frubber

Wide-angled camera mounted in chest gives Sophia a view of the room.

SOPHIA

A SMART FUTURE?

No one knows quite how smart robots will become in the future, but it's certain there will be advances in how they sense, make decisions and operate. Robots and other machines are likely to become much more common and more involved in people's lives.

300,000,000 ...

... the number of driverless vehicles predicted to be on the world's roads in 2050.

TECHNICAL ADVANCES

Advances in technology could help make robots more intelligent and useful. Better batteries could allow mobile and social robots to operate for longer periods between recharges. New, smart materials, may lead to robots which can change shape to perform different tasks.

KNOW-IT-ALLS

Faster connectivity may lead to robots being able to access almost unlimited stores of data about you. Future personal robots may be able to offer all kinds of help, at work and play.

More intelligent sensors and controllers could enable robots to work with each other closely in 'lights-out' factories – free of humans so there's no need for lighting or heating.

50 ...

... the estimated number of big robots built each day by robots in FANUC's lights-out factory in Japan. Human staff only visit once every 600 working hours to check if maintenance is needed.

FURHAT

Dimensions: 41 cm x 27 cm x 24 cm

Weight: 3.5 kg

Microphones: 4

Camera: 1 x 120° wide angle

Lights 88 x LEDs

IT'S BEEN EMOTIONAL

Future social robots may look, act and seem to think more like humans than versions do today. They will be better at reading humans' feelings, understanding conversations and responding in suitable ways. Some may even look like Furhat - a prototype robot head from Sweden which uses AI to have meaningful chats with people. Its face is moulded but the unlimited facial expressions it can form are optical, cast onto it by a projector.

QUIZ

Try this quiz to find out how much you can remember about super-smart robots. The answers are at the bottom of the page.

1. In which country was the 2019 RoboCup tournament held?

a) Australia

b) Japan

c) Slovakia

2. How many legs does the ANYmal C have?

a) Two

b) Four

c) Six

3. What is the name of the humanoid robot made a UN ambassador in 2017?

a) Sophia

b) Jian Lailai

c) Baxter

4. How long is the Cimon-2 robot's mission in space planned to last?

a) Six months

b) One year

c) Three years

5. How many sensors will you find in a NAO robot?

a) More than 20

b) More than 35

c) More than 50

6. Who was the human world chess champion that the IBM Deep Blue computer beat in 1997?

a) Magnus Carlsen

b) Garry Kasparov

c) Bobby Fischer

7. How many lines of computer code are used to run the robot iCub?

a) 500,000

b) 1,500,000

c) 4,000,000

8. How many cameras are used in a Waymo driverless car?

a) 12

b) 29

c) 67

9. Which robot, built by Cynthia Breazeal, had 15 degrees of freedom and could express nine emotions?

a) Kismet

b) Ai-Da

c) Leka

10. How far did the Stanley driverless car navigate by itself in 2005?

a) 36 km

b) 142 km

c) 281 km

GLOSSARY

autonomous
Describes a machine that can make decisions and works by itself.

cloud computing
The storage of data and use of apps and programs on computers accessed over the Internet.

computer network
Two or more computers linked together so they can exchange messages and data.

controller
The part of the robot which makes decisions and tells the other parts of the robot what to do. It is usually a computer.

database
An organised collection of information that allows data to be easily searched and retrieved.

degrees of freedom
The different ways and directions in which a robot or its parts can move.

evaporate
To turn from a liquid into a gas.

feedback
Useful information about a situation or how a task is going, sent back to the robot by its sensors.

Global Positioning System (GPS)
A navigation system using a series of satellites orbiting Earth to give an accurate position on Earth.

humanoid
Describes a robot that has a partial or complete human-like appearance or one that performs human-like actions.

infrared
A type of electromagnetic radiation, like light, but not visible to our eyes.

LiDAR
Short for Light Detection And Ranging, this is a sensor system that sends out pulses of laser light to measure distances to objects.

prototype
A first version of a device made to test it out or to raise publicity.

sensor
A device that collects information about a robot or its surroundings.

supercomputer
A particularly powerful, high-performance computer used for exceptionally complex tasks.

ultrasonic
Describes sound waves that exist above the range of human hearing.

FURTHER INFORMATION

Books

A Robot World – Clive Gifford, Franklin Watts, 2019

Explore AI: Intelligent Robots – Sonya Newland, Wayland, 2021

The Tech-Head Guide: AI – William Potter, Wayland, 2021

Websites

https://www.youtube.com/watch?v=kB5Bg2277Pg&index=70&list=PLslScfOUDB71T4yQqtCXCdviViNigDBap
See ASIMO and two other advanced humanoid robots in action.

https://www.youtube.com/watch?v=KTpRiPFbmuE
See how iCub learns about objects and compares it to others with this BBC video.

https://www.youtube.com/watch?v=5_jp9CwJhcA
Watch the social robot Sophia answer questions in an interview.

INDEX

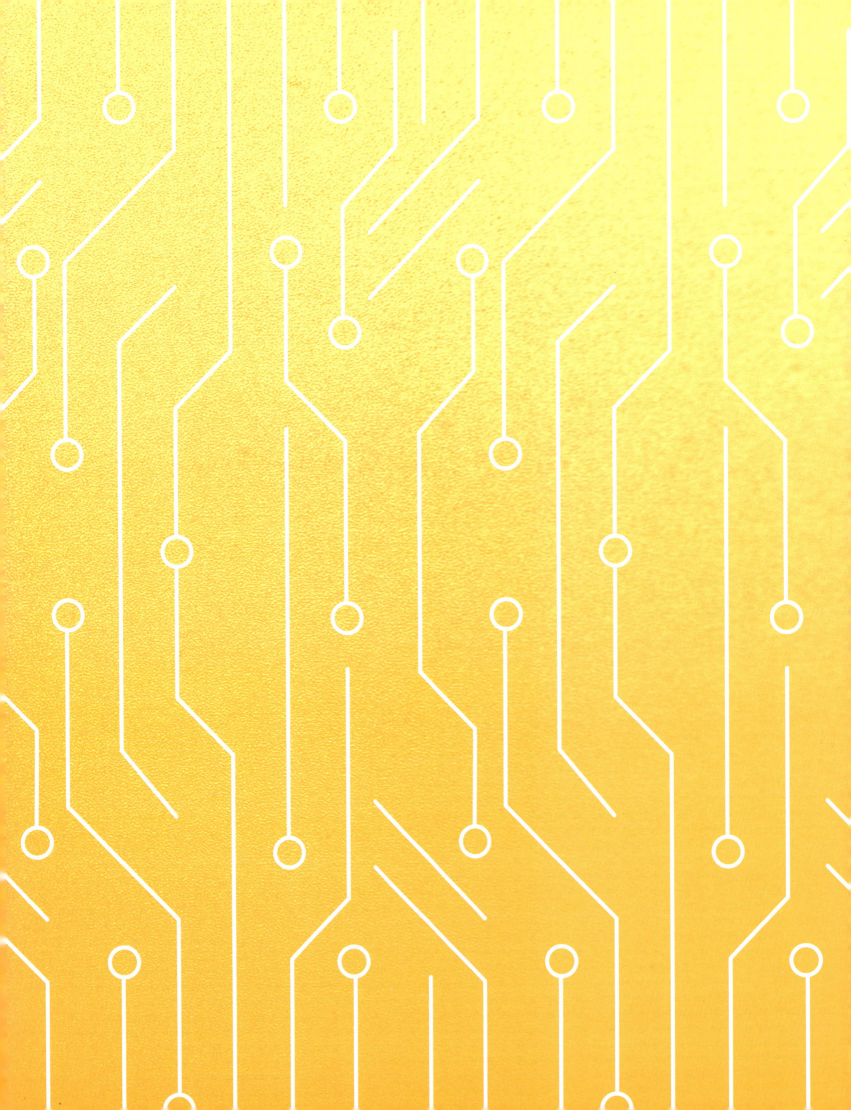